Yellow in My World

By Brienna Rossiter

level
1
little blue
readers

www.littlebluehousebooks.com

Little Blue House is distributed by North Star Editions:
sales@northstareditions.com | 888-417-0195

Produced for Little Blue House by Red Line Editorial.

Photographs ©: Shutterstock Images, cover, 4, 7, 9, 13, 14–15, 16 (top left), 16 (top right), 16 (bottom right); iStockphoto, 10–11, 16 (bottom left)

Library of Congress Control Number: 2020900746

ISBN
978-1-64619-162-8 (hardcover)
978-1-64619-196-3 (paperback)
978-1-64619-264-9 (ebook pdf)
978-1-64619-230-4 (hosted ebook)

Printed in the United States of America
Mankato, MN
082020

About the Author

Brienna Rossiter enjoys playing music, reading books, and drinking tea. She lives in Minnesota.

Table of Contents

I See Yellow

The leaf is yellow.

The bus is yellow.

The sign is yellow.

The chair is yellow.

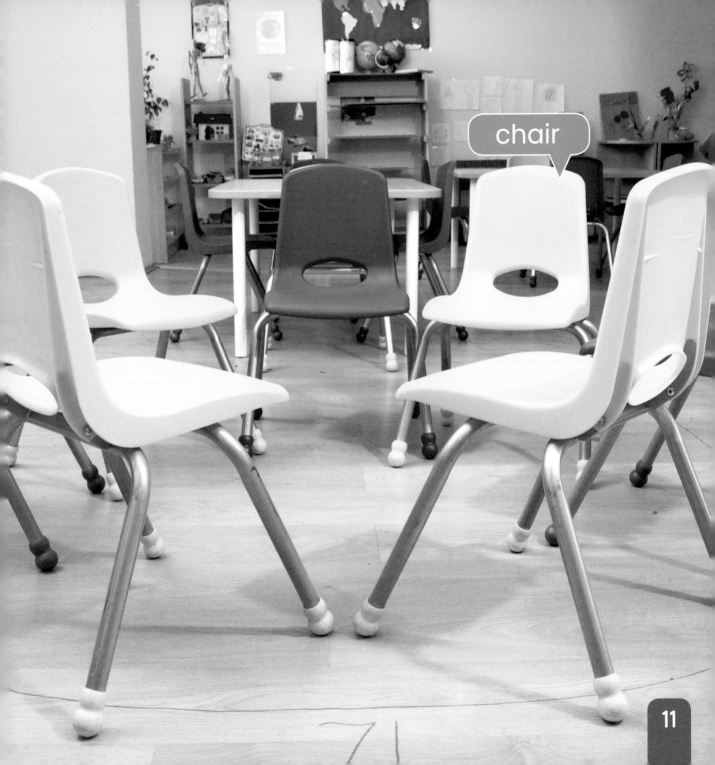

chair

11

The banana is yellow.

The wall is yellow.

Glossary

banana

leaf

chair

sign

Index